Steck-Vaughn
Shutterbug Books
SCIENCE

Animal Eyes

by Ellen Catala

STECK-VAUGHN
Harcourt Supplemental Publishers

www.steck-vaughn.com

Animals live in oceans, deserts, jungles, and forests.
Wherever there are animals, there are animal eyes.
They are looking, watching, searching, finding.

Seeing helps animals find food and avoid danger.
Some animals use their sense of sight almost all the time.
Others depend more on their senses of hearing or smell.

Eagles have amazing eyesight.

An eagle can spot a meal from very high up in the sky.

An eagle swoops down and catches its prey—almost never missing its target!

Leopards also use their eyes to hunt.

Leopards hunt mostly at night, when there is little light.

A special part in their eyes helps them see in the dark.

The part makes the leopard's eyes seem to glow!

Bushbabies also see well at night.
During the day, the openings in their eyes close up into slits.
But at night, they open up wide and round.
This helps them see in the dark.

Squid eyes can be as wide as car headlights!
Squids know how to make it hard for their enemies to see.
When in danger, they squirt an inky liquid into the water.
Hidden by this dark cloud, they make their escape.

Eyes that stick out help an animal to see all around.

A rabbit freezes when it senses danger.

It stays perfectly still, moving only its eyes.

A rabbit can see all around without moving its head.

An alligator's eyes help it see without being seen. The eyes of an alligator stick up high on its head. When underwater, an alligator can poke its eyes up and look around.

Chameleons look in different directions at the same time.
One eye looks one way, while the other looks another way.
What does the world look like to a chameleon?
No one really knows.

Crab eyes are made up of many parts.

Every part sees a slightly different picture.

To a crab, the whole world looks like a giant puzzle!

Ostriches have two sets of eyelids.

One set is made of skin, with very long eyelashes.

The other eyelids are clear and close upward.

They protect the eyes while letting the ostrich see.

Some geckos have no eyelids.

They cannot blink to keep their eyes wet.

Instead, they have to lick them with their tongues!

Most spiders trap their food in webs.
But jumping spiders hunt for their prey.
To do this, they need very good eyesight.

Animal eyes can be big or small, in the front, or on the side.
Wherever they are, they are watching.
Are they watching you?

Index